Why I Can't Save

Why I Can't Save

Matthew Petchinsky

1

Why I Can't Save: Trauma Blocks to Financial Planning

By: Matthew Petchinsky

Disclaimer

This book, ***Why I Can't Save: Trauma Blocks to Financial Planning*****, is a creative, educational, and psychological exploration of the emotional, neurological, and trauma-based barriers that interfere with saving money, planning ahead, or maintaining financial stability.**

It is **not** a substitute for professional financial advice, therapy, legal guidance, or mental-health treatment.

The insights, frameworks, and explanations in this book are designed to help readers **understand internal resistance**, identify hidden survival responses, and explore how trauma shapes money behaviors. While the book discusses financial themes, it does so **through the lens of emotional patterning, behavioral psychology, trauma responses, and nervous system dynamics—not through investment strategy or professional planning standards.**

All exercises, reflections, techniques, and tools provided throughout the book are **educational suggestions only**. They are meant to foster insight and self-awareness, not to direct or dictate your financial decisions. Every reader's financial situation, trauma history, emotional capacity, and available resources are different. Any choices you make regarding budgeting, savings, spending, or financial planning should be made at your own discretion and, when appropriate, in consultation with a licensed financial advisor, therapist, counselor, or other qualified professional.

The author makes **no guarantees** regarding financial results, behavioral outcomes, or emotional transformation. Healing trauma and creating new money patterns is a personal, nonlinear process that unfolds over time.

For crisis situations—financial, emotional, or otherwise—please reach out to a qualified professional or emergency service in your area.

This book is offered with care, respect, and the intention to support your growth, self-understanding, and empowerment. Use what resonates, release what does not, and trust your pace as you navigate your own healing and financial evolution.

Introduction

For trauma survivors, the idea of "later" often feels unsafe. The future isn't a calm horizon you move toward—it's a place where things have gone wrong before. When you have lived through instability, emergencies, neglect, poverty, or unpredictable environments, your nervous system learns one message with brutal clarity: **"Survive now. Worry about everything else later."**

This book begins with a truth that is rarely spoken in traditional financial conversations:

If you struggle to save money, you are not lazy, irresponsible, or "bad with money."

You are responding exactly as your mind and body were trained to respond during the hardest chapters of your life.

Trauma does not care about interest rates, budgets, or long-term goals. Trauma cares only about safety. And the future—abstract, distant, and uncertain—can feel like a threat. Trauma makes "later" feel dangerous. It trains you to focus on the next hour, the next meal, the next crisis. It creates a financial identity shaped not by choice, but by survival.

Many people say, "Saving is simple: just put money away."

But if your past taught you that money disappears, that emergencies strike without warning, or that every moment of stability eventually collapses, saving can feel psychologically impossible—even when you desperately want to.

This book offers a compassionate explanation for something you may have blamed yourself for your entire life. We are diving into the emotional blocks, brain patterns, and survival defenses that make planning feel overwhelming. You will learn how trauma interferes with executive function, long-term thinking, emotional regulation, and your relationship to money. You will see why your reactions make sense, how they developed, and why they have nothing to do with moral failure.

But this book is not about staying stuck in old patterns.
It is about **making peace with planning**—not overnight, not perfectly, but gently and realistically. As you explore the deeper roots of your financial resistance, you will learn practical tools for building safety in your body, clarity in your mind, and stability in your habits. Instead of forcing yourself to "be better with money," you will learn how to make saving feel safe for the first time.

You are not broken.
Your brain simply learned to survive unpredictable worlds.
Now, together, we will learn how to build a future that feels solid—not frightening.

Welcome to a new chapter of financial healing.

Chapter 1 — The Future Isn't Safe: Trauma Time Distortions

Trauma reshapes time. It fractures the threads that connect "now" to "later," turning tomorrow into something hazy, threatening, or unreachable. For trauma survivors, the future is not a gentle landscape where dreams rest—it is a place where things have historically gone wrong. Stability hasn't lasted. Safety hasn't held. Promises have been broken. Crisis arrived without warning.

So your nervous system learned to live in a constant state of **compressed time**—a world where the present moment expands to fill everything, and the future collapses into fog. This distortion deeply affects saving, planning, consistency, and anything that requires delayed reward.

Understanding trauma's impact on time is the first step in healing your relationship with money.

Trauma Trains the Body to Prioritize Immediate Survival

When you grow up—or live for long periods—in environments of chaos, neglect, instability, or chronic fear, the brain adapts by becoming hyper-attuned to the present. The amygdala (your threat detector) takes the lead, pushing your nervous system into survival mode.

In this state, the brain prioritizes:

- **Immediate relief over delayed benefits**
- **Short-term safety over long-term security**
- **Quick escape over slow building**

Saving money requires trusting that the future will come and that your efforts will matter when it does. But trauma conditions the body to believe the opposite: that the next danger will arrive before you ever benefit from saving. It becomes emotionally safer to spend now than to prepare for a future your nervous system doesn't trust.

When the Past Repeats Itself Inside the Present

Trauma survivors often have a split perception of time. On one hand, the past feels painfully close—like it's still happening. On the other hand, the future feels far away, abstract, and unreal. This creates a sense of being stuck in "forever now."

If you grew up hearing things like:

- "Who knows where we'll be tomorrow."
- "Don't count on anything."
- "Everything falls apart eventually."
- "We might not make it that long."

Then planning wasn't just difficult—it was dangerous. Imagining the future set you up for disappointment. Hoping made you vulnerable. Saving money would have felt pointless, even unsafe, because the world around you taught you that nothing lasts.

The child or teenager inside you still carries that message.

Time Scarcity and Emotional Dysregulation

Trauma causes the brain to collapse all time into the urgency of right now. This creates a constant low-grade panic: *If I don't meet my needs immediately, something bad will happen.*

This is called **time scarcity**, and it:

- Shrinks your ability to plan
- Overwhelms executive function
- Makes future-oriented tasks feel impossible
- Creates impulsive spending habits
- Triggers self-blame when long-term goals crumble

This has nothing to do with discipline.

It is physiology.

Your nervous system is trying to protect you based on outdated—but once necessary—survival strategies.

Trauma Disconnects You From "Future You"

Saving requires empathy for your future self—an understanding that who you will be next month or next year deserves care and resources.

Trauma interrupts this. You may:

- Struggle to picture your future self
- Feel emotionally disconnected from them
- Not trust that you'll still be okay by then
- Believe that survival today matters more than comfort tomorrow
- Feel guilt or fear imagining a better life

When you can't emotionally *feel* your future self, you can't naturally save for them.

This is not irresponsibility—it's trauma severing the internal thread that links today to tomorrow.

The Unspoken Fear: "What If I Never Get to Use What I Save?"

One of the most common—but least discussed—trauma responses is the silent fear that planning for the future is a waste of time.

If life has taught you that:

- Good things don't last
- You don't get to enjoy the rewards
- Safety falls apart quickly
- Crisis always arrives
- You lose things you care about

Then saving money can trigger fear instead of hope.

You may subconsciously think:

"Why would I save something that life will just take away from me?"

And so spending now feels safer—consistent with what your nervous system learned.

Rebuilding a Safe Relationship With the Future

Healing financial trauma is not about spreadsheets, budgets, or strict rules. It begins with repairing your sense of time and rebuilding emotional safety around the idea of "later."

Little by little, you learn:

- That the future is not just a threat
- That stability can grow over time
- That your needs matter beyond today
- That saving is a form of protection, not punishment
- That your future self deserves support

The work starts here—by understanding that your difficulty saving has a root cause, and it is valid, human, and treatable.

Grounding Exercise: "Reclaiming the Next Ten Minutes"

Trauma makes the future feel enormous, terrifying, and unsafe. This exercise shrinks "the future" into a tiny, safe window your brain can handle.

How to do it:

1. Sit or lie down comfortably.
2. Place one hand on your chest and one on your stomach.
3. Say out loud:
   "I only need to handle the next ten minutes. That's all."
4. Name three things you will do in the next 10 minutes:
    - drink water
    - breathe slowly
    - rest for a moment
5. Then say:
   "The next ten minutes are safe."

Purpose:

This teaches your brain that the future can be broken into small, manageable moments instead of overwhelming years.

Somatic Breathing Technique: The 4–2–6 Trauma Reset

Use whenever thinking about saving or planning triggers anxiety.

1. Inhale for **4** seconds.
2. Hold for **2** seconds.
3. Exhale slowly for **6** seconds.
4. Repeat **8 times**.

Why it works:

The long exhale signals the parasympathetic nervous system ("we're safe now"), reducing time-based panic.

Reflection Exercise: "Mapping My Time Safety Zones"
Draw three circles and label them:

- **Past Me**
- **Present Me**
- **Future Me**

Inside each circle, write:

- how that version of you feels
- what that version fears
- what that version needs

Purpose:
This repairs the fractured sense of time trauma creates and helps unify your internal identities.

Practical Tip: The One-Minute Planning Rule
A gentle introduction to planning **without triggering fear**:
Every day, take **one minute** to do one micro-plan:

- Decide one thing you'll eat tomorrow.
- Decide one task for tomorrow.
- Decide one self-care action tomorrow.

This shows your nervous system that planning can be tiny, safe, and non-threatening.

Micro-Saving Step: "The Trauma-Safe Savings Jar"
You create **three categories**:

1. **Today Me**
2. **Tomorrow Me**
3. **Someday Me**

Place **1–5 cents** in each. Yes—cents.

Why it works:
Your brain begins to emotionally bond with the idea that the future deserves resources *without depriving the present.*
This is trauma-safe savings.

10 Journal Prompts

1. When I think about the future, what emotions rise first—fear, numbness, hope, anxiety, avoidance? Why?
2. What did I learn about "the future" from my childhood, caregivers, or past relationships?
3. Do I trust that my future self will be safe, alive, and able to enjoy what I save? Why or why not?
4. What does "later" feel like in my body? Tightness, heaviness, fogginess, panic, nothingness?
5. In what areas of my life do I feel stuck in survival mode?
6. When have I been punished—emotionally or literally—for planning or hoping?
7. How has instability shaped my relationship with money?
8. What would it feel like if the future were safe for me? Describe it in detail.
9. How does the idea of saving money make me feel physically and emotionally?
10. What would a compassionate first step toward planning look like for me—not perfect, not big, just kind?

Closing Reflection

Time becomes distorted when trauma shapes it. If you have struggled to save, plan, or imagine the future, it is not because you are flawed—it is because your nervous system has been surviving conditions that demanded constant vigilance. This chapter is the beginning of a gentle reconnection with "later." You do not have to trust the future immediately. You do not have to feel confident in planning today. You only have to begin noticing how time feels inside your body.

As you move forward through this book, remember:

Healing financial trauma is not about forcing discipline.
It is about reclaiming safety—one small moment at a time.

When you reshape your relationship with time, you reshape your relationship with money. And more importantly, you reshape your relationship with yourself.

Chapter 2 — Why Saving Feels Like Self-Abandonment

For many trauma survivors, saving money triggers a surprising emotional reaction: guilt, fear, resistance, or even panic. Not because saving is bad—but because it can feel like abandoning your present self in order to protect a future version of you that feels distant, unreal, or undeserving. Saving requires putting resources away where you can't touch them, denying yourself something now so that someone—"Future You"—benefits later.

But when you've lived through trauma, especially poverty, neglect, instability, or emotional deprivation, **your present self has been the one left behind over and over again**. Needs went unmet. Comfort was postponed indefinitely. You were told, directly or indirectly, that who you were "right now" didn't matter.

So when saving tells you, "Not now," your nervous system hears an old wound:

"You don't matter again."

This chapter explores why saving doesn't just feel difficult—it feels personal.

Immediate Needs Were Never Safe to Ignore

When you grow up or live in survival mode, your present needs are not optional or flexible—they are emergencies. Hunger, fear, unstable housing, financial volatility, and emotional unpredictability all teach the body one core belief:

"If I don't take care of myself right now, no one will."

Saving money requires delaying comfort.

Delaying comfort requires trusting that:

- you will still be safe later
- your needs won't explode into crisis
- someone (you) will take care of you when the moment arrives

But trauma survivors often have a history of being punished for delaying needs. Ignoring what you needed today didn't lead to a reward later—it led to more suffering. So your brain learned that withholding resources from yourself is dangerous.

Not spending money today can feel like re-enacting that neglect.

Trauma Creates a Divided Self: "Present Me" vs. "Future Me"

Most financial advice assumes one unified person who cares about every version of themselves.

But trauma fragments the internal timeline.

There is:

- **The Present Self** who is exhausted, overwhelmed, and craving relief
- **The Past Self** who was denied, ignored, or hurt
- **The Future Self** who feels unreal, unreachable, or undeserving

To save money, you must trust and value your future self. But if trauma taught you that:

- the future never arrives
- nothing lasts
- you won't get to enjoy stability
- emergencies destroy everything you build
- plans collapse in the last minute

...then future-you doesn't feel like a safe investment.

Instead, you cling to the present version of yourself—the only one who has ever reliably *needed* you. Saving money becomes emotionally coded as "hurting today-me for the sake of someone who might not even exist."

Logically, you may know that isn't true.

Emotionally, it feels like a betrayal.

Saving Can Trigger Old Patterns of Being Deprived

Many trauma survivors have lived through deeply painful experiences of deprivation:

- being told "we don't have money" during childhood
- having to give up small pleasures out of survival
- growing up where every purchase felt shameful
- being controlled financially by others
- being denied things out of punishment
- experiencing scarcity for long stretches of life

When you try to save, you may unconsciously re-create that same emotional deprivation:

"No, you can't have that."
"You don't need anything."
"You're asking for too much."
"Stop wanting so much."

Saving activates the part of you that once suffered because your needs were minimized.

It doesn't matter that the deprivation now comes from you with good intentions—it still feels like an old wound reopening.

When Saving Feels Like You're Leaving Your Inner Child Behind

Inside every trauma survivor is an inner child who remembers the moments when they needed comfort and no one came. That part of you still exists—raw, sensitive, and alert to any sign that you're neglecting yourself again.

So when you choose to save instead of easing discomfort today, your inner child may feel:

- abandoned
- ignored
- punished
- dismissed
- unsafe
- unheard

This inner-child reaction can be subtle but powerful. It can show up as:

- sudden urges to spend
- physical anxiety
- emotional overwhelm
- guilt for withholding anything
- shame for "not taking care of yourself"
- self-sabotage ("I already messed up; might as well spend it all")

Your adult mind may say, "Saving is smart and responsible,"
but your trauma-patterned mind says, "Why are you doing this to me again?"

Unless we address this emotional layer, saving will always feel like self-neglect.

The Emotional Cost of Delayed Comfort

One of the biggest myths about trauma survivors is that they overspend because they "lack control."

The truth is much deeper:

Comfort is not a luxury for traumatized people—it is a lifeline.

Comfort regulates the nervous system.
Comfort signals safety.
Comfort restores a sense of dignity.
Comfort shrinks the pain of old wounds.

So when saving asks you to give up comfort *today*, it can feel like stripping away your only source of relief. This makes saving feel like emotional self-harm, even when you logically know it's necessary.

For someone who has been deprived, comfort is not frivolous—it is survival.

This is why trauma survivors often associate saving with:

- emotional starvation
- returning to past suffering
- recreating patterns of neglect
- being "the responsible one" while others hurt them
- making themselves small again

Your brain may resist saving not because you are irresponsible, but because saving feels like betraying the part of you that desperately needs safety *right now*.

Reframing Saving: From Self-Abandonment to Self-Protection

Healing begins with understanding: you are not actually choosing between present-you and future-you. You are trying to reconnect two parts of yourself that trauma separated.

You can begin to shift saving into a form of **self-care**, not punishment, by:

- Creating safety around small "micro savings"
- Making saving feel comforting, not depriving
- Reassuring your inner child each time you save
- Treating future-you as a real, living version of you—not a stranger
- Allowing yourself to enjoy things *and* save without guilt
- Building emotional trust before financial structure

This chapter does not ask you to save big yet.
It asks you to understand why saving has felt like a threat—to your identity, your past, your emotional safety, and your sense of self-worth.

When you heal this wound, saving becomes an act of loyalty rather than abandonment.

Inner Child Connection Ritual: "I Won't Leave You Behind"
Do this before saving money or making plans.

1. Place your hand on your heart.
2. Close your eyes and picture your younger self.
3. Say:
   "I'm not taking anything away from you. I'm taking care of you—now and later."
4. Imagine giving your inner child a small, comforting object.
5. Tell them:
   "You matter today AND tomorrow."

Purpose:
This prevents saving from feeling like emotional deprivation.

Somatic Release Exercise: "Permission to Need Things"

Saving often triggers guilt for wanting comfort. This exercise interrupts that guilt.

1. Stand or sit with your shoulders relaxed.
2. Take a slow breath in.
3. As you exhale, whisper:
   "I'm allowed to have needs."
4. Repeat while gently shaking out your hands or feet to release stored tension.

Embodied Visualization: "Future Me is Real"

Picture your future self **6 months from now**, not years. Imagine:

- what they wear
- how they feel
- what they are relieved about
- how they benefit from the tiny savings you do today

Then say:

"I'm not abandoning myself—I'm supporting myself."

Practical Tip: The 50/50 Comfort-Saving Formula
To avoid feeling deprived:
Every time you want to spend, do this:

- **Half goes to comfort today**
- **Half goes to comfort later**

Examples:

- Want a $10 treat? Spend $5, save $5.
- Want a $4 snack? Buy it, then save $4 cents in your jar.
- Want a $50 indulgence? Buy something for $25 instead and save $25.

Purpose:
It makes saving feel like a partnership, not punishment.

Micro-Saving Step: The "Gentle Coin Promise"
Pick one coin you save **every day**:

- 1 penny
- 1 nickel
- 1 dime

This is symbolic—not financial.
It's about telling your nervous system:
"Saving won't hurt you."
This builds emotional safety around saving.

10 Journal Prompts

1. When I choose to save instead of spend, what emotions come up for me?
2. Does saving feel like I'm denying myself something I need? Why?
3. What messages did I receive growing up about wanting, needing, or asking?
4. When did I first learn that my needs were inconvenient or "too much"?
5. Does my "inner child" feel cared for or ignored when I try to save?
6. What small comforts feel essential for my emotional safety today?
7. How have I been deprived in the past, and how does that influence spending now?
8. What would it feel like to treat saving as a gift to myself instead of a punishment?
9. How do I feel about the idea of being kind to both my present and future self?
10. What is one tiny, non-threatening way I could begin saving without triggering fear?

Closing Reflection

Saving money becomes emotionally complicated when you have survived environments where your needs were dismissed, ignored, or belittled. What looks like "irresponsibility" from the outside is often a profound internal struggle between the part of you that needed comfort *yesterday* and the part of you trying to build safety for tomorrow.

You have never been wrong for wanting comfort now.
You have never been wrong for wanting relief.

This chapter is an invitation to stop punishing yourself for the ways trauma taught you to cope. You are not abandoning yourself by learning to save. You are gently reconnecting the fractured parts of your identity—the child who suffered, the adult who is surviving, and the future self who is waiting to feel cared for.

Saving becomes possible not through discipline, but through healing.

You deserve safety in every timeline of your life.

Chapter 3 — From Impulse to Inner Calm

Impulsive spending isn't a character flaw—it's a nervous system response. For trauma survivors, impulse isn't merely a "lack of control." It is a coping mechanism that provided survival, relief, or protection during times when life felt overwhelming or unpredictable. Your impulses were never random; they were your body's attempt to create safety in a world that didn't feel safe.

In this chapter, we unpack how trauma wires your brain for urgency, why your impulses spike under pressure, and how you can slowly shift from impulsive reactions into a grounded, centered inner calm that makes saving and planning feel possible.

Impulses Are Nervous System Fire Alarms

When the nervous system is overwhelmed, it seeks to regulate itself by reducing emotional discomfort as fast as possible. This creates the emotional equation:

Overwhelm → Impulse → Temporary Relief

Trauma survivors often experience:

- chronic stress
- emotional exhaustion
- hypervigilance
- dissociation
- panic spikes
- sudden drops in energy
- shame or self-blame

Your brain learns that a quick purchase gives:

- distraction
- dopamine
- comfort
- control
- a sense of agency
- a momentary escape from fear or sadness

These moments of relief are not about material objects—they are about **soothing the alarm inside your nervous system**.

This is why impulsive spending feels automatic: the impulse happens before the thinking part of your brain (prefrontal cortex) can even activate.

You were never weak. You were overwhelmed.

Trauma Disrupts the Ability to Pause

People often give simplistic advice like:

"Just stop and think."

"Stick to your budget."

"Walk away and come back later."

But trauma survivors often cannot pause when triggered. Trauma rewires the brain for speed, not reflection.

When you have lived through environments where:

- hesitation was dangerous
- slow decisions led to harm
- thinking things through caused punishment
- you had to act fast to protect yourself
- emotional overwhelm hit like a tidal wave

...your brain learned that **pausing is unsafe**.

So it pushes you toward action—any action—to regain control.

Impulses weren't a failure.

They were your survival reflex.

Impulsive Purchases Are Often Bids for Emotional Stability

What you buy impulsively carries clues about your emotional wounds:

- **Comfort items** → needing safety
- **Food** → soothing deprivation or emptiness
- **Self-care products** → longing to be cared for
- **Gifts for others** → trying to earn love or avoid rejection
- **Random items** → trying to feel alive, stimulated, or distracted
- **Small indulgences** → trying to reclaim dignity
- **Big purchases** → attempting to prove worth or power

Every impulse has a psychological story behind it.

It was never about money.

It was about relief.

When you understand the emotional need behind the impulse, you gain the power to meet that need in healthier ways—without shame, without self-punishment, and without fear.

Inner Calm Begins With Emotional Safety, Not Rules

Traditional financial advice starts with behavior: budgets, restrictions, systems.

Trauma healing starts with the opposite: **safety**.

You cannot expect a dysregulated nervous system to behave like a calm one. So before you think about controlling impulses, you must create an inner environment where your body feels grounded enough that you don't need them as much.

Inner calm comes from:

- nervous system regulation
- naming what you feel
- grounding exercises
- deep self-compassion
- small choices that build internal trust
- recognizing when you are triggered
- creating micro-moments of safety

Impulse reduction is a *side effect* of emotional grounding—not the main goal.

Learning to Intercept Impulse with Curiosity, Not Shame

Shame intensifies impulses.
Curiosity dissolves them.

When you notice the urge to spend, instead of saying:

"What's wrong with me?"
"Why can't I stop doing this?"
"I'm sabotaging again."

Try asking:

"What emotion is underneath this?"
"What pain am I trying to soothe?"
"What doesn't feel safe right now?"
"What need is going unmet?"
"What am I craving emotionally—not materially?"

When you approach impulses with curiosity, the nervous system softens. The urgency decreases. The mind becomes clearer. You shift from acting *inside* the impulse to observing it from *outside*.

This is where inner calm begins.
Not with control.
With compassion.

Micro-Calm: Small Steps to Regulate Your Nervous System Before You Spend

You don't need huge habits to change your relationship with impulse—you need **micro-calming rituals** that take 10–30 seconds.

Examples:

- place one hand on your chest and take a slow breath
- press your feet firmly into the ground
- put your phone down for 20 seconds
- ask yourself "what am I feeling right now?"
- relax your shoulders intentionally
- drink a slow sip of water
- stretch your arms and release tension
- place your hand on your belly to feel your breath

These micro-calming actions interrupt the impulse long enough for your brain to return to clarity.

Over time, you will find that you need fewer impulse-driven behaviors because your body learns to regulate itself gently.

This is how financial healing begins: one grounded moment at a time.

Impulse Interruption Technique: "The 20-Second Safety Pause"

Before acting on an impulse, do this:

1. Put both feet flat on the ground.
2. Inhale for 4 seconds.
3. Exhale for 6 seconds.
4. Place one hand on your belly.
5. Say:
   "I'm safe enough to pause."

Purpose:

It interrupts the panic-driven adrenaline rush that creates impulse spending.

Emotion Naming Practice: "Label Before You Spend"
When an impulse hits, ask:

- Am I lonely?
- Am I bored?
- Am I scared?
- Am I tired?
- Am I seeking comfort?
- Am I overwhelmed?

Then say:
"I'm not buying something. I'm trying to soothe something."
Naming emotion decreases impulse power by up to 40%.

Body-Based Technique: "The Softening Scan"
A 30-second grounding technique.

1. Relax your shoulders.
2. Unclench your jaw.
3. Uncurl your toes.
4. Loosen your stomach.
5. Soften your gaze.

Impulses lose intensity when the body exits the fight/flight state.

Practical Tip: The One-Hour Wishlist

Create a note in your phone called:

"The Later List."

When an impulse hits, write it there.

Promise yourself:

"If I still want this after one hour, I can revisit it."

Most impulses fade once the nervous system calms.

Micro-Saving Step: The "If I Don't Buy It, I Save It" Rule

When you resist an impulse—even a small one—save the smallest unit possible instead:

- 1 penny
- 5 cents
- 10 cents
- $1 if possible

This transforms resisting impulses into a small reward.

Over time, your brain associates calming down with **gaining** something, not losing something.

10 Journal Prompts

1. What situations or emotions tend to trigger my impulsive spending the most?
2. What unmet need am I usually trying to soothe when I buy something quickly?
3. When I act on impulse, what physical sensations happen in my body?
4. Which purchases in the past were actually attempts to regulate my emotions?
5. How did my childhood environment teach me to act fast instead of pausing?
6. What does "inner calm" mean to me personally?
7. What small moments of safety can I create during my day?
8. What types of purchases give me temporary relief but long-term stress?
9. What would a compassionate response to my impulses look like?
10. How can I remind myself that slowing down is safe for me now?

Closing Reflection

Impulse is not the enemy—it is a messenger. It tells you when you're overwhelmed, when your inner child is frightened, when your nervous system is strained, and when you're carrying emotional pain alone. Every impulse has meaning. Every urge has a history. And every moment of internal chaos is an opportunity to learn, soften, and heal.

As you continue this journey, remember:

You don't overcome impulses by force.
You transform them through safety.

Inner calm doesn't erase your trauma history—it gently rewires your relationship to it. Over time, as you build trust with your own body, saving will no longer feel like deprivation. Planning will no longer feel like punishment. Calm will become the new language of your nervous system.

Your impulses were born from survival.
Your calm will come from healing.

Chapter 4 — Safe Future Visualization Rituals

For trauma survivors, the future has never felt like a safe place. It may feel blank, threatening, foggy, or painfully unreal. Visualizing tomorrow can trigger fear. Imagining next year can trigger panic. Thinking about five years from now can feel impossible, even dangerous.

This isn't lack of ambition.
This isn't irresponsibility.
This is trauma.

When the past has taught you that stability collapses, people disappear, chaos returns, or plans fall apart, your nervous system will naturally recoil from future imagery. This chapter is about gently rebuilding your brain's ability to imagine a future that is not terrifying—one that is **possible**, **stable**, **caring**, and **safe**.

Safe future visualization rituals help reconnect the parts of you that trauma disconnected: who you were, who you are, and who you are becoming. They help transform the future from a threat into a companion.

The Problem: The Future Activates Old Survival Wounds

Traditional self-help says:
"Visualize your dream life."
But trauma survivors often feel:

- nothing
- numbness
- fear
- blank mental space
- sadness
- confusion
- overwhelm
- pressure

The future feels like something you must *survive*, not something you can *enter with confidence*. This is because the future carries associations with:

- abandonment
- uncertainty
- instability
- poverty
- danger
- loss
- disappointment
- repeated trauma cycles

Your brain tries to protect you by stopping you from looking too far ahead.

This chapter teaches your nervous system how to gently **open a window into a safe future**, not a forced one.

Safe Visualization Rituals vs. Traditional Visualization

Most visualization practices are too intense for trauma survivors because they demand:

- clarity
- certainty
- emotional excitement
- big goals
- long-term trust

Trauma-informed visualization is the opposite. It focuses on:

- feeling safe
- staying grounded
- imagining small, believable scenarios
- connecting to stability, not pressure
- repairing the emotional link between today and "later"

You are not visualizing success.
You are visualizing safety.

This distinction matters.

When the future feels safe, success can grow naturally.

Safe Future Ritual #1: The "Tomorrow Morning" Visualization

This is the most trauma-safe ritual because it avoids overwhelming time distances.

How to Do It:

1. Sit comfortably and place your feet flat on the ground.
2. Take one slow breath, in and out.
3. Imagine yourself **waking up tomorrow**.
4. Picture only:
    - the room
    - the light
    - your breath
    - the feeling of waking up gently
5. Say:
   "I will meet myself tomorrow."

Why it works:
It rebuilds your connection to the very next version of yourself—something trauma tends to sever.

Safe Future Ritual #2: "Three Hours Ahead" Grounding
For when the future feels too big.

1. Look at a clock.
2. Count **three hours forward** from the present moment.
3. Picture yourself doing something simple:
    - sitting on your couch
    - drinking water
    - writing in your journal
    - resting
4. Place your hand on your chest and say:
   "The future is small enough to hold."

Purpose:
This shrinks time into something that feels manageable.

Safe Future Ritual #3: The "Six-Month Sanctuary Scene"

This is the first visualization that introduces distance—gently. Sit with your eyes closed and imagine:

- a safe place
- a calm environment
- a room with soft light
- a relaxed version of you sitting peacefully
- the feeling of comfort in your body

Do **not** imagine goals.
Do **not** imagine achievements.
Only safety.

Say:

"Safety is allowed in my future."

Purpose:

This builds emotional trust with future-you.

Safe Future Ritual #4: The "Continuity Ribbon" Meditation
This meditation repairs the sense that time is fragmented.
Steps:

1. Close your eyes.
2. Imagine today-you holding a soft ribbon.
3. See your future self (one month ahead) holding the other end.
4. Slowly imagine the ribbon becoming strong, warm, connected.
5. Say:
   "We are connected.
   I don't abandon you, and you don't abandon me."

Purpose:
It heals the psychological break between present and future identity.

Safe Future Ritual #5: Micro-Saving Visualization
A savings ritual that *doesn't trigger deprivation*:

1. Hold a coin, even a penny.
2. Look at it in your hand.
3. Whisper:
   "This is for the version of me who survives this moment."
4. Place the coin somewhere safe.
5. Visualize your future self smiling softly—not excited, just relieved.

Purpose:
Saving becomes an act of care, not punishment.

Trauma-Safe Savings Practices

The "Soft Plan" Technique

Instead of strict goals, use:

- "I might save a little."
- "I'll see what feels safe tomorrow."
- "I can save without hurting myself."
- "Saving can be gentle."

This language reduces pressure and prevents shutdown.

The "Comfort-First Savings Method"
Before saving anything:

- drink water
- take a breath
- relax shoulders
- regulate your body

Only save *after* you feel grounded.
This prevents saving from triggering fear or deprivation.

The "Two Futures" Technique
Picture:

- **Unsafe future:** the old trauma-based story
- **Safe future:** a new possibility

Then tell your brain:
"I choose the second one."
This re-trains future imagery toward safety.

10 Journal Prompts

1. When I imagine the future, what emotions arise first?
2. What did my childhood or past experiences teach me about tomorrow?
3. Does the idea of the future feel threatening, blank, or overwhelming? Why?
4. What tiny future moment feels safe enough to imagine right now?
5. How does my body react when I think about next month or next year?
6. What would a safe future look like—not perfect, just safe?
7. What parts of myself fear the future the most?
8. What would it feel like if future-me trusted me more?
9. How can I create comfort in the present before visualizing the future?
10. What is one ritual from this chapter I can try this week?

Closing Reflection

You are not broken for fearing the future. You are not weak for avoiding it. You learned to protect yourself in the only way you could—by collapsing time and staying close to the present moment.

This chapter is not about forcing big dreams.
It is about gently introducing the possibility that tomorrow might not hurt you.

Future-you is not a stranger.
Future-you is a survivor waiting for your care.

When you approach visualization through safety instead of pressure, the future becomes less threatening. And as safety grows, planning grows. Saving grows. Hope grows.

This is how healing begins:
one soft vision, one gentle breath, one safe tomorrow at a time.

Chapter 5 — Trauma-Aware Saving Systems

Saving money is often taught like a discipline problem—something you fix with stronger rules, tighter budgets, or more "willpower." But for trauma survivors, saving is not a discipline issue. It is a **nervous system issue**, a safety issue, a history issue, and a trust issue. Trauma-aware saving systems don't force discipline; they build emotional security. They work *with* your body, not against it. They don't ask you to leap into the future—they invite you to walk there gently.

This chapter is the bridge between emotional healing and practical financial systems. It brings everything together: safety, compassion, visualization, impulse regulation, and inner calm. What you build here is not a budget. It is a relationship—with yourself, your money, and your future.

Why Traditional Saving Systems Fail Trauma Survivors

Traditional financial advice assumes that people:

- trust the future
- feel safe delaying gratification
- have stable emotional regulation
- don't panic under pressure
- can pause before acting
- don't experience deprivation wounds
- can easily visualize long-term outcomes

Trauma survivors cannot use systems built on these assumptions.

Because trauma creates:

- time distortions
- future-blindness
- survival urgency
- emotional depletion
- deprivation triggers
- fear of losing control
- self-worth wounds
- abandonment fears (even from future-you)

A trauma survivor trying to use a traditional savings system is like a person with a broken leg being told to "just run harder." The system isn't wrong—it's just not designed for your nervous system.

Trauma-aware saving systems repair safety first, then saving second.

The Foundation: Safety Before Systems

A trauma-aware saving system begins with three emotional truths:

1. Saving must feel safe.

If saving feels threatening, your brain will sabotage it.

2. Saving must feel small.

Tiny amounts allow your body to stay regulated.

3. Saving must feel self-loving, not self-abandoning.

You cannot save for a future self you resent, fear, or cannot imagine.

These truths form the foundation of every tool in this chapter.

Trauma-Aware Saving System #1: "Micro-Deposits for Micro-Safety"

This is the core of trauma-aware saving:

Save amounts so small the nervous system doesn't panic.

Examples:

- 1¢
- 5¢
- 10¢
- 25¢
- $1 only if it feels safe

Why it works:

The amount is not the point—the *practice* is.
You are teaching your brain:

- saving is not dangerous
- you will not suffer for saving
- the present is still cared for
- the future receives gentle support

Micro-saving slowly rewires your trauma responses around money.

Trauma-Aware Saving System #2: The 3-Part Safety Jar Ritual
Label three jars:

1. **Today Me**
2. **Tomorrow Me**
3. **Future Me**

Each time you save:

- put **something tiny** in all three (1–5 cents)
- say aloud:
  "No version of me is left behind."

Why this works:
It heals the abandonment wound at the root of money trauma.

Trauma-Aware Saving System #3: Comfort-Linked Saving

To prevent the emotional deprivation trigger:

Whenever you save:

- drink something warm
- wrap up in a blanket
- breathe deeply
- light a candle
- hold your heart

Combine saving with soothing.

This re-associates saving with comfort—not punishment—which rewires the trauma bond.

Trauma-Aware Saving System #4: The "Impulse Conversion" Technique

When an impulse to spend hits:

1. Pause using a grounding breath.
2. Name the emotion driving the impulse.
3. Instead of buying the item, save **the smallest amount** (1–10 cents).
4. Say:
   "I am choosing calm, not crisis."

This practice transforms impulses into empowerment.

Trauma-Aware Saving System #5: The "Slow Plan" Method
Instead of budgeting by month or year, use:

- **Tomorrow**
- **The Next 10 Minutes**
- **This Afternoon**
- **This Week**

Tiny planning windows prevent overwhelm and shutdown.
Example:

- Tomorrow: save 10 cents
- This week: choose one comfort ritual
- In 10 minutes: breathe and stretch

This builds planning tolerance without threatening the nervous system.

Trauma-Aware Saving System #6: The Safe Future Envelope
Write an envelope titled:
"For the Me Who Survives This."
Place inside:

- one penny
- or one dollar (only if safe)
- or a handwritten note about a future comfort you deserve

This creates emotional continuity between versions of yourself fractured by trauma.

Trauma-Healing Tools for This Chapter

Somatic Tool: "The Safety Anchor Touch"
Use before saving:

1. Place your hand on your belly.
2. Take a slow breath.
3. Whisper:
   "I am safe while I save."

This reduces anxiety spikes.

Meditation: "Meeting Tomorrow Me"
A two-minute visualization.

1. Close your eyes.
2. Picture yourself *tomorrow morning* safe in bed.
3. Imagine handing tomorrow-you one penny.
4. See them smile softly.
5. Whisper:
   "I take care of you now."

This repairs the future-self disconnect.

Breathing Technique: The 7-Second Soft Exhale

1. Inhale for 4.
2. Exhale for 7.
3. Repeat five times.

This calms amygdala-driven urgency surrounding money.

Practical Tip: The 3-Item Survival Budget
Instead of a full budget, list the **three things** that matter most:

- food
- comfort
- one bill

Anything beyond that is optional.
This prevents overwhelm while still building structure.

Micro-Saving Step: "The Soft Cent Ritual"

Every night before bed:

Save **one penny**.

Say:

"I'm healing this slowly and safely."

This ritual becomes a nightly nervous system repair.

10 Journal Prompts

1. What emotions do I feel when I think about saving money?
2. Which saving system from this chapter feels the safest to try first?
3. What past experiences made saving feel threatening or painful?
4. How does my body react when I separate money for the future?
5. What tiny saving action feels completely non-threatening?
6. How can I combine saving with comfort instead of deprivation?
7. What does "financial safety" mean to me—not success, just safety?
8. What version of me (past, present, future) needs reassurance around saving?
9. What is one small way I can connect with future-me this week?
10. How do I want saving to feel in my body one year from now?

Closing Reflection

Trauma changes your relationship with money—not because you are broken, but because you survived environments where safety came second to survival. This book has carried you through the emotional landscape of time distortion, self-abandonment wounds, impulse fire-alarms, and fear of the future. Now, this final chapter gives you the systems to heal through saving—not by force, but by gentleness.

You are not learning to save the traditional way.
You are learning to save the **trauma-aware way**:

- Softly
- Slowly
- Safely
- In tiny amounts
- With compassion
- With your nervous system
- With your inner child
- And with your future self

Every cent becomes a message:

“I choose safety. I choose care. I choose continuity. I choose me.”

This is not the end of your financial healing—this is the beginning of a future where saving is not punishment, but self-love.

Appendix A — Safe-Saving Templates

Trauma-aware saving is never about perfection, pressure, or discipline. It is about safety, connection, and emotional pacing. These templates are designed to help you save in small, compassionate ways that work with your nervous system—not against it.

Use them exactly as written, or adapt them to whatever feels safe. Even one penny saved with safety is more healing than $100 saved with fear.

These templates fall into five categories:

1. **Daily Micro-Saving Templates**
2. **Weekly Trauma-Safe Saving Systems**
3. **Impulse-Conversion Saving Templates**
4. **Visualization-Based Saving Templates**
5. **Future-Self Connection Saving Templates**

Let's begin.

Section 1 — Daily Micro-Saving Templates

Gentle, non-triggering practices for daily safety-building.

Template 1: The "Soft Cent" Ritual (Nightly Saving)

When to use: Every night before bed, or anytime you're tired, overwhelmed, or anxious.

Materials:

- 1 penny
- A small cup/jar/envelope
- A quiet moment

Steps:

1. Place your hand on your heart and breathe once—slow, not forced.
2. Whisper:
   "I save gently. I save safely."
3. Drop *one* penny into the jar.
4. Close your eyes for 3 seconds.
5. Say:
   "Future-me will receive this with gratitude."

Why it works:

This creates micro-consistency without triggering deprivation or fear.

Optional Variation:

If a penny feels too much during bad days, tap the jar lightly instead. The ritual still counts.

Template 2: The 3-Jar Safety Deposit

When to use: Morning or evening, especially when feeling emotionally fragmented.

Materials:

- Three small cups or jars labeled:
    1. **Today Me**
    2. **Tomorrow Me**
    3. **Future Me**

Steps:

1. Place 1–5 cents in each jar.
2. As you place each coin, speak aloud:

Today Me:
"You are safe. I take care of you first."

Tomorrow Me:
"I will meet you with compassion."

Future Me:
"I won't abandon you anymore."

Why it works:
It repairs the inner split trauma creates between past, present, and future selves.

Template 3: Body-Based Saving
When to use: When saving triggers body tension.
Steps:

1. Relax shoulders.
2. Loosen your jaw.
3. Inhale for 4, exhale for 7.
4. Place 1–10 cents into your saving spot.
5. Say:
   "My body stays calm while I save."

Why it works:
Saving becomes paired with physical calm instead of panic.

Section 2 — Weekly Trauma-Safe Saving Systems
For readers ready for slightly more structure without pressure.

Template 4: The Weekly Soft Goal Check-In
When to use: Once a week, no guilt allowed.
Materials:

- A notebook
- 5–10 minutes
- A grounding breath

Steps:

1. Start by writing:
   "Saving is not a test. Saving is an experiment."
2. Write down:
    - How saving felt this week
    - What was easy
    - What was hard
    - What triggered fear
3. Save **only** what feels safe today.
4. Close with this affirmation:
   "I am building trust, not perfection."

Template 5: The Gentle Week Envelope
When to use: Sundays or any calm day.
Materials:

- One envelope
- Optional: a comforting scent or sticker

Steps:

1. Choose any amount that feels non-threatening (1 penny to $1).
2. Place it inside the envelope.
3. Seal it while breathing slowly.
4. Write on the envelope:
   "This is for my calm, stable future."

Why it works:
It makes saving sensory, comforting, and grounding.

Template 6: The "Comfort Pairing" Weekly Ritual

Saving must never feel like punishment. This ritual links saving with comfort.

Steps:

1. Make something soothing (tea, warm water, cozy blanket).
2. Sit somewhere peaceful.
3. Save a tiny amount (10 cents–$1).
4. Enjoy the comfort for at least 2 minutes afterward.

Why it works:

It rewires the brain to associate saving with soothing, not deprivation.

Section 3 — Impulse-Conversion Saving Templates
Perfect for moments when emotions spike and spending urges rise.

Template 7: The "Pause, Name, Save" System
Steps:

1. When an impulse hits, pause for one breath.
2. Name the emotion:
    - fear
    - boredom
    - loneliness
    - shame
    - overwhelm
3. Save a small amount (1–10 cents).
4. Say:
   "I choose calm instead."

Why it works:
It transforms a moment of emotional intensity into empowerment.

Template 8: The One-Hour Wishlist
When to use: During online browsing or shopping temptation.
Steps:

1. Write the item in a note titled **"Maybe Later."**
2. Set a timer for 1 hour.
3. After the hour, ask:
    - Do I still want it?
    - What emotion was this impulse feeding?
4. Save something small instead (penny to $1).

Variation:

If the impulse is too strong, simply breathe and do NOT force saving. Safety first.

Template 9: The $0.25 Crisis Conversion
When a trauma trigger makes you want to spend:

1. Hold a coin in your hand.
2. Close your eyes.
3. Let your breath deepen.
4. Place the coin into your safe jar.
5. Whisper:
   "Crisis doesn't control me anymore."

Section 4 — Visualization-Based Saving Templates
For readers who engage visually or emotionally.

Template 10: The "Safe Tomorrow" Visualization Deposit
Steps:

1. Picture yourself tomorrow in a safe, calm moment.
2. Hand future-you a coin in that visualization.
3. Place that same coin in your jar in real life.
4. Breathe once.
5. Say:
   "I will meet you safely tomorrow."

Template 11: The "Six-Month Sanctuary" Save
When you feel stable enough to imagine a future:

1. Visualize a peaceful scene six months ahead.
2. Imagine setting down a small object (coin, stone, note).
3. Save a matching coin in real life.
4. Write one sentence:
   "Safety grows slowly."

Template 12: The Ribbon Continuity Saving Practice
Steps:

1. Visualize today-you holding one end of a ribbon.
2. Visualize future-you (any distance you choose) holding the other end.
3. Save a tiny amount.
4. Imagine the ribbon glowing gently.
5. Say:
   "We stay connected."

Section 5 — Future-Self Connection Saving Templates

For repairing the relationship between present-you and future-you.

Template 13: The "Letter to Future Me" Savings Envelope

Steps:

1. Write a short, kind note to your future self.
2. Include statements like:
    - "I won't abandon you."
    - "This is for your comfort."
    - "You deserve stability."
3. Save something tiny (a coin or $1).
4. Seal both inside an envelope.

Template 14: The 3-Minute Inner Child & Future Self Dialogue

Steps:

1. Close your eyes.
2. Visualize your inner child.
3. Visualize your future self.
4. Let them speak gently to each other.
5. Save any small amount afterward.

Purpose:

This bridges the gap between past trauma and future healing.

Template 15: The "Future Me Fund"

This is the most advanced template in the entire appendix.

Steps:

1. Create a dedicated jar or account titled:
   "For the Me Who Survives This Chapter."
2. Save what feels safe—nothing more.
3. Write a note each time describing how saving felt.
4. Read past notes monthly to build continuity.

Closing Reflection

You did something extraordinary by reaching the end of this appendix. Not because you mastered every template, and not because you saved a certain amount—but because you stayed present with yourself while exploring a completely new way of relating to money, safety, and your future.

Trauma reshapes the nervous system so profoundly that even the smallest acts—saving a penny, taking a breath before spending, imagining tomorrow—can feel immense. Every template in this appendix honors that truth. These rituals are not about building wealth quickly or forcing discipline. They are about building safety: a safety you may have never been given, a safety you are now learning to create from within.

Each tiny action you take, each cent you save, each moment you breathe before acting is not just a financial choice—it is a message to every past version of yourself who felt abandoned, deprived, or unseen. It says:

"I am here now. I am not leaving you behind. We can build this together."

These templates are tools, but more than that, they are bridges—bridges between your present self and your future self, between survival patterns and healing patterns, between the person you had to be and the person you are becoming.

There is no right pace and no wrong pace.

There is only your pace.

Your rhythm.

Your healing.

Whether you use one template or ten, whether you save a penny or a dollar, whether you do these rituals daily or occasionally, the most important thing is that you approach each step with gentleness. Trauma-aware saving is built not on pressure, but on compassion. Not on perfection, but on connection.

Remember:

- **Safety comes first.**
- **Consistency grows slowly.**
- **Self-trust develops over time.**
- **Every tiny step matters.**

You do not have to force your way into financial healing.

You can **walk softly**, save gently, and let safety lead the way.

This appendix is not an ending—it is an invitation.

A doorway into a future where saving doesn't hurt, where planning doesn't overwhelm you, and where every version of you—past, present, and future—finally gets to feel cared for.

You are building something sacred: not just savings, but self-security.

Not just a future, but a future that feels safe to step into.

Appendix B — Future Self Connection Journal

The relationship between your present self and your future self has been fractured by trauma, survival mode, deprivation, and fear. These journal prompts are designed to help you reconnect to who you are becoming—slowly, softly, without pressure or perfection.

You do not need to complete all 100.
You do not need to finish them in order.
Move at your own pace.
Use them as invitations, not requirements.

Gentle Introductions to Future You

These prompts are soft, accessible, and non-threatening.

1. What is one thing I hope future-me feels every morning?
2. What small comfort do I want future-me to have that I don't have now?
3. What is something future-me no longer worries about?
4. What do I want future-me to remember about today?
5. How do I hope future-me speaks to themselves?
6. What is the kindest thing I can imagine future-me saying to me right now?
7. What do I want future-me to thank me for?
8. What do I hope future-me knows about my struggles today?
9. What gentle strength do I want future-me to carry?
10. What does a safe morning look like for future-me?
11. In what ways do I hope future-me feels more grounded?
12. What is one tiny ritual future-me practices daily?
13. What is one thing I hope future-me has let go of?
14. What soft boundary do I hope future-me has in place?
15. How does future-me show themselves compassion?
16. What is future-me's ideal way to rest?
17. What does "safety" feel like in future-me's body?
18. What is future-me passionate about?

19. How does future-me celebrate small victories?
20. What is one thing I want future-me to never forget about who I am right now?

Building Emotional Trust With Future You

These prompts gently strengthen emotional continuity.

1. What fears do I want future-me to be free from?
2. How does future-me comfort their inner child?
3. What new belief about money does future-me hold?
4. What emotional courage do I want future-me to develop?
5. What brings future-me peace on difficult days?
6. What does future-me forgive me for?
7. What do I hope future-me no longer feels ashamed about?
8. What habits help future-me stay calm?
9. How does future-me speak to themselves during stressful moments?
10. What does future-me do when they feel overwhelmed?
11. What is one kind thing future-me does for their body?
12. What is one kind thing future-me does for their nervous system?
13. What new emotional boundaries does future-me practice?
14. How has future-me healed from money trauma?
15. What does future-me want to reassure me about?
16. What part of my identity has grown in future-me?
17. How does future-me respond to fear differently than I do now?
18. What is a fear future-me wants me to release?
19. What emotional wounds has future-me softened?
20. What brings future-me comfort when life feels uncertain?

Rewriting the Future Narrative

Prompts that help reclaim the future as something possible, safe, and compassionate.

1. What does a safe afternoon look like for future-me?
2. What does a calm financial moment look like for future-me?
3. What small luxury or comfort has future-me allowed themselves to enjoy?
4. What routine brings future-me stability?
5. What relationships feel safe for future-me?
6. What kind people are around future-me?
7. What is the gentlest version of my ideal future?
8. What is future-me learning right now?
9. What helps future-me feel secure when plans change?
10. What simple pleasure does future-me savor?
11. How does future-me rest without guilt?
12. What does future-me's evenings look like?
13. What daily rituals help future-me feel anchored?
14. What emotionally healthy behaviors does future-me practice naturally?
15. What brings future-me quiet joy?
16. What does financial calm look like for future-me?
17. What has future-me stopped apologizing for?
18. What gentle boundaries does future-me hold with others?
19. What new opportunities feel safe for future-me?
20. What does future-me cherish most about life?

Healing Money Trauma Through Connection

These prompts deepen the relationship between your nervous system and future financial safety.

1. What is future-me's relationship with money like?
2. What does saving feel like in future-me's body?
3. What messages about money has future-me rewritten?
4. How does future-me soothe money anxiety?
5. What belief does future-me hold about their worthiness of stability?
6. How does future-me spend intentionally without shame?
7. What feels emotionally safe for future-me to save for?
8. How does future-me celebrate financial progress?
9. What trauma responses around money has future-me healed?
10. What does financial peace look like to future-me?
11. What financial fears no longer control future-me?
12. How does future-me approach long-term planning safely?
13. What money habits help future-me feel grounded?
14. What does future-me want to tell me about saving gently?
15. What emotions does future-me feel when they look at their savings jar?
16. What emotional beliefs about scarcity has future-me released?
17. What makes future-me trust money more?
18. What makes future-me trust themselves more?
19. How does future-me show gratitude for small savings?
20. What does financial healing mean to future-me?

Becoming the Version of You Who Feels Safe Existing

These final prompts anchor identity, hope, safety, and inner continuity.

1. Who is future-me when they feel fully safe?
2. What makes future-me proud of me today?
3. What qualities in future-me are beginning to form now?
4. How does future-me nourish themselves emotionally?
5. What does future-me believe about their future that I struggle to believe now?
6. What inner strengths does future-me use daily?
7. What does future-me know about healing that I don't yet?
8. What brings future-me a feeling of inner security?
9. In what ways is future-me more gentle with themselves?
10. What has future-me learned to enjoy without fear?
11. What identity has future-me stepped into?
12. What does future-me wish I could trust more deeply?
13. What message of reassurance does future-me want to give me?
14. What truth does future-me live that I am only beginning to understand?
15. What does future-me appreciate about the person I am now?
16. How does future-me safeguard their energy and peace?
17. What has future-me forgiven themselves for?
18. What new emotional freedom does future-me experience?
19. What is the most surprising thing about future-me?
20. If future-me could wrap me in a feeling, what would that feeling be?

Closing Reflection

You have just completed one of the most important parts of this book—not because you answered every prompt, and not because you wrote the "right" things, but because you allowed yourself to begin a conversation with someone trauma once taught you to ignore: **your future self.**

For many survivors, the future feels unreachable, unreal, or unsafe. It can feel like a place where pain repeats itself, where stability collapses, or where you are alone again. These prompts were never about dreaming big or imagining a perfect life. They were about something far more meaningful:

rebuilding the trust that trauma took from your timeline.

Each question you answered—or even paused to consider—was an act of courage. You reached forward. You reached inward. You showed your nervous system that "later" can exist without danger, without disappointment, without fear. You created emotional continuity where survival mode once created fragmentation.

The future you are connecting with does not need to be extraordinary. They just need to be **safe**, **steady**, and **present**. Someone who enjoys waking up in their own skin. Someone who feels calm when they look at their savings—no matter the amount. Someone who understands their needs and honors their limits. Someone who feels possible.

If these prompts stirred emotions, softened something inside you, or made you pause to breathe, that is the deepest form of healing. If they felt difficult or overwhelming, that is healing too—because it means you met a part of yourself that has long been waiting for gentleness.

Remember this:

The future you are writing toward is not a stranger.
They are you—just with a little more safety, a little more softness, and a little more room to breathe.

You don't have to rush to meet them.
You don't have to become them overnight.

You just have to keep walking toward them in small, compassionate steps.

With every prompt you complete, you weave a thread between the person you are today and the person you will one day be. This thread is fragile at first, but with time, it becomes strong enough to carry hope, savings, self-trust, and emotional security.

Your future self is waiting with open arms—not with judgment, but with gratitude.

You are no longer walking into the future alone.
You are walking toward a version of you who already believes in you.

<u>Message from the Author:</u>

I hope you enjoyed this book, I love astrology and knew there was not a book such as this out on the shelf. I love metaphysical items as well. Please check out my other books:

-Life of Government Benefits

-My life of Hell

-My life with Hydrocephalus

-Red Sky

-World Domination:Woman's rule

-World Domination:Woman's Rule 2: The War

-Life and Banishment of Apophis: book 1

-The Kidney Friendly Diet

-The Ultimate Hemp Cookbook

-Creating a Dispensary(legally)

-Cleanliness throughout life: the importance of showering from childhood to adulthood.

-Strong Roots: The Risks of Overcoddling children

-Hemp Horoscopes: Cosmic Insights and Earthly Healing

- Celestial Hemp Navigating the Zodiac: Through the Green Cosmos

-Astrological Hemp: Aligning The Stars with Earth's Ancient Herb

-The Astrological Guide to Hemp: Stars, Signs, and Sacred Leaves

-Green Growth: Innovative Marketing Strategies for your Hemp Products and Dispensary

-Cosmic Cannabis

-Astrological Munchies

-Henry The Hemp

-Zodiacal Roots: The Astrological Soul Of Hemp

- **Green Constellations: Intersection of Hemp and Zodiac**

-Hemp in The Houses: An astrological Adventure Through The Cannabis Galaxy

-Galactic Ganja Guide

Heavenly Hemp

Zodiac Leaves
Doctor Who Astrology
Cannastrology
Stellar Satvias and Cosmic Indicas
Celestial Cannabis: A Zodiac Journey
AstroHerbology: The Sky and The Soil: Volume 1
AstroHerbology:Celestial Cannabis:Volume 2
Cosmic Cannabis Cultivation
The Starry Guide to Herbal Harmony: Volume 1
The Starry Guide to Herbal Harmony: Cannabis Universe: Volume 2
Yugioh Astrology: Astrological Guide to Deck, Duels and more
Nightmare Mansion: Echoes of The Abyss
Nightmare Mansion 2: Legacy of Shadows
Nightmare Mansion 3: Shadows of the Forgotten
Nightmare Mansion 4: Echoes of the Damned
The Life and Banishment of Apophis: Book 2
Nightmare Mansion: Halls of Despair
Healing with Herb: Cannabis and Hydrocephalus
Planetary Pot: Aligning with Astrological Herbs: Volume 1
Fast Track to Freedom: 30 Days to Financial Independence Using AI, Assets, and Agile Hustles
Cosmic Hemp Pathways
How to Become Financially Free in 30 Days: 10,000 Paths to Prosperity
Zodiacal Herbage: Astrological Insights: Volume 1
Nightmare Mansion: Whispers in the Walls
The Daleks Invade Atlantis
Henry the hemp and Hydrocephalus

10X The Kidney Friendly Diet
Cannabis Universe: Adult coloring book
Hemp Astrology: The Healing Power of the Stars

Zodiacal Herbage: Astrological Insights: Cannabis Universe: Volume 2

Planetary Pot: Aligning with Astrological Herbs: Cannabis Universes: Volume 2

Doctor Who: Convergence Protocol – The Replicator War

Nightmare Mansion: Curse of the Blood Moon

The Celestial Stoner: A Guide to the Zodiac

Cosmic Pleasures: Sex Toy Astrology for Every Sign

Hydrocephalus Astrology: Navigating the Stars and Healing Waters

Lapis and the Mischievous Chocolate Bar

Celestial Positions: Sexual Astrology for Every Sign

Apophis's Shadow Work Journal: **:** A Journey of Self-Discovery and Healing

Kinky Cosmos: Sexual Kink Astrology for Every Sign

Digital Cosmos: The Astrological Digimon Compendium

Stellar Seeds: The Cosmic Guide to Growing with Astrology

Apophis's Daily Gratitude Journal

Cat Astrology: Feline Mysteries of the Cosmos

The Cosmic Kama Sutra: An Astrological Guide to Sexual Positions

Unleash Your Potential: A Guided Journal Powered by AI Insights

Whispers of the Enchanted Grove

Cosmic Pleasures: An Astrological Guide to Sexual Kinks

369, 12 Manifestation Journal

Whisper of the nocturne journal(blank journal for writing or drawing)

The Boogey Book

Locked In Reflection: A Chastity Journey Through Locktober

Generating Wealth Quickly:How to Generate $100,000 in 24 Hours

Star Magic: Harness the Power of the Universe

The Flatulence Chronicles: A Fart Journal for Self-Discovery

The Doctor and The Death Moth

Seize the Day: A Personal Seizure Tracking Journal

The Ultimate Boogeyman Safari: A Journey into the Boogie World and Beyond

Whispers of Samhain: 1,000 Spells of Love, Luck, and Lunar Magic: Samhain Spell Book

Apophis's guides:Witch's Spellbook Crafting Guide for Halloween

Frost & Flame: The Enchanted Yule Grimoire of 1000 Winter Spells

The Ultimate Boogey Goo Guide & Spooky Activities for Halloween Fun

Harmony of the Scales: A Libra's Spellcraft for Balance and Beauty

The Enchanted Advent: 36 Days of Christmas Wonders

Nightmare Mansion: The Labyrinth of Screams

Harvest of Enchantment: 1,000 Spells of Gratitude, Love, and Fortune for Thanksgiving

The Boogey Chronicles: A Journal of Nightly Encounters and Shadowy Secrets

The 12 Days of Financial Freedom: A Step-by-Step Christmas Countdown to Transform Your Finances

Sigil of the Eternal Spiral Blank Journal

A Christmas Feast: Timeless Recipes for Every Meal

Holiday Stress-Free Solutions: A Survival Guide to Thriving During the Festive Season

Yu-Gi-Oh! Holiday Gifting Mastery: The Ultimate Guide for Fans and Newcomers Alike

Holiday Harmony: A Hydrocephalus Survival Guide for the Festive Season

Celestial Craft: The Witch's Almanac for 2025 – A Cosmic Guide to Manifestations, Moons, and Mystical Events

Doctor Who: The Toymaker's Winter Wonderland

Tulsa King Unveiled: A Thrilling Guide to Stallone's Mafia Masterpiece

Pendulum Craft: A Complete Guide to Crafting and Using Personalized Divination Tools

Nightmare Mansion: Santa's Eternal Eve

Starlight Noel: A Cosmic Journey through Christmas Mysteries

The Dark Architect: Unlocking the Blueprint of Existence

Surviving the Embrace: The Ultimate Guide to Encounters with The Hugging Molly

The Enchanted Codex: Secrets of the Craft for Witches, Wiccans, and Pagans

Harvest of Gratitude: A Complete Thanksgiving Guide

Yuletide Essentials: A Complete Guide to an Authentic and Magical Christmas

Celestial Smokes: A Cosmic Guide to Cigars and Astrology

Living in Balance: A Comprehensive Survival Guide to Thriving with Diabetes Insipidus

Cosmic Symbiosis: The Venom Zodiac Chronicles

The Cursed Paw of Ambition

Cosmic Symbiosis: The Astrological Venom Journal

Celestial Wonders Unfold: A Stargazer's Guide to the Cosmos (2024-2029)

The Ultimate Black Friday Prepper's Guide: Mastering Shopping Strategies and Savings

Cosmic Sales: The Astrological Guide to Black Friday Shopping

Legends of the Corn Mother and Other Harvest Myths

Whispers of the Harvest: The Corn Mother's Journal

The Evergreen Spellbook

The Doctor Meets the Boogeyman

The White Witch of Rose Hall's SpellBook

The Gingerbread Golem's Shadow: A Study in Sweet Darkness

The Gingerbread Golem Codex: An Academic Exploration of Sweet Myths

The Gingerbread Golem Grimoire: Sweet Magicks and Spells for the Festive Witch

The Curse of the Gingerbread Golem

10-minute Christmas Crafts for kids

Christmas Crisis Solutions: The Ultimate Last-Minute Survival Guide

Gingerbread Golem Recipes: Holiday Treats with a Magical Twist

The Infinite Key: Unlocking Mystical Secrets of the Ages

Enchanted Yule: A Wiccan and Pagan Guide to a Magical and Memorable Season

Dinosaurs of Power: Unlocking Ancient Magick

Astro-Dinos: The Cosmic Guide to Prehistoric Wisdom

Gallifrey's Yule Logs: A Festive Doctor Who Cookbook

The Dino Grimoire: Secrets of Prehistoric Magick

The Gift They Never Knew They Needed

The Gingerbread Golem's Culinary Alchemy: Enchanting Recipes for a Sweetly Dark Feast

A Time Lord Christmas: Holiday Adventures with the Doctor

Krampusproofing Your Home: Defensive Strategies for Yule

Silent Frights: A Collection of Christmas Creepypastas to Chill Your Bones

Santa Raptor's Jolly Carnage: A Dino-Claus Christmas Tale

Prehistoric Palettes: A Dino Wicca Coloring Journey

The Christmas Wishkeeper Chronicles

The Starlight Sleigh: A Holiday Journey

Elf Secrets: The True Magic of the North Pole

Candy Cane Conjurations

Cooking with Kids: Recipes Under 20 Minutes

Doctor Who: The TARDIS Confiscation

The Anxiety First Aid Kit: Quick Tools to Calm Your Mind

Frosty Whispers: A Winter's Tale

The Infinite Key: Unlocking the Secrets to Prosperity, Resilience, and Purpose

The Grasping Void: Why You'll Regret This Purchase

Astrology for Busy Bees: Star Signs Simplified

The Instant Focus Formula: Cut Through the Noise

The Secret Language of Colors: Unlocking the Emotional Codes

Sacred Fossil Chronicles: Blank Journal

The Christmas Cottage Miracle

Feeding Frenzy: Graboid-Inspired Recipes

Manifest in Minutes: The Quick Law of Attraction Guide

The Symbiote Chronicles: Doctor Who's Venomous Journey

Think Tiny, Grow Big: The Minimalist Mindset

The Energy Key: Unlocking Limitless Motivation

New Year, New Magic: Manifesting Your Best Year Yet

Unstoppable You: Mastering Confidence in Minutes

Infinite Energy: The Secret to Never Feeling Drained

Lightning Focus: Mastering the Art of Productivity in a Distracted World

Saturnalia Manifestation Magick: A Guide to Unlocking Abundance During the Solstice

Graboids and Garland: The Ultimate Tremors-Themed Christmas Guide

12 Nights of Holiday Magic

The Power of Pause: 60-Second Mindfulness Practices

The Quick Reset: How to Reclaim Your Life After Burnout

The Shadow Eater: A Tale of Despair and Survival

The Micro-Mastery Method: Transform Your Skills in Just Minutes a Day

Reclaiming Time: How to Live More by Doing Less

Chronovore: The Eternal Nexus

The Mind Reset: Unlocking Your Inner Peace in a Chaotic World

Confidence Code: Building Unshakable Self-Belief

Baby the Vampire Terrier
Baby the Vampire Terrier's Christmas Adventure
Celestial Streams: The Content Creator's Astrology Manual
The Wealth Whisperer: Unlocking Abundance with Everyday Actions
The Energy Equation: Maximize Your Output Without Burning Out
The Happiness Algorithm: Science-Backed Steps to Joyful Living
Stress-Free Success: Achieving Goals Without Anxiety
Mindful Wealth: The New Blueprint for Financial Freedom
The Festive Flavors of New Year: A Culinary Celebration
The Master's Gambit: Keys of Eternal Power
Shadowed Secrets: Groundhog Day Mysteries
Beneath the Burrow: Lessons from the Groundhog
Spring's Whispers: The Groundhog's Prediction
The Limitless Mindset: Unlock Your Untapped Potential
The Focus Funnel: How to Cut Through Chaos and Get Results
Bold Moves: Building Courage to Live on Your Terms
The Daily Shift: Simple Practices for Lasting Transformation
The Quarter-Life Reset: Thriving in Your 20s and 30s
The Art of Shadowplay: Building Your Own Personal Myth
The Eternal Loop: Finding Purpose in Repetition
Burrowing Wisdom: Life Lessons from the Groundhog
Shadow Work: A Groundhog Day Perspective
Love in Bloom: 5-Minute Romantic Gestures
The Shadowspell Codex: Secrets of Forbidden Magick
The Burnout Cure: Finding Balance in a Busy World
The Groundhog Prophecy: Unlocking Seasonal Secrets
Nog Tales: The Spirited History of Eggnog
Six More Weeks: Embracing Seasonal Transitions
The Lumivian Chronicles: Fragments of the Fifth Dimension
Money on Your Mind: A Beginner's Guide to Wealth
The Focus Fix: Breaking Through Distraction

January's Spirit Keepers: Mystical Protectors of the Cold
Creativity Unchained: Unlocking Your Wildest Ideas in 2025
Manifestation Mastery: 365 Days to Rewrite Your Reality
The Groundhog's Mirror: Reflecting on Change
The Weeping Angels' Christmas Curse
Burrowed in Time: A Groundhog Day Journey
Heartbeats: Poems to Share with Your Valentine
Dino Wicca: The Sacred Grimoire of Prehistoric Magick
Courage of the Pride: Finding Your Inner Roar
The Lion's Leap: Bold Moves for Big Results
Healthy Hustle: Achieving Without Overworking
Practical Manifesting: Turning Dreams into Reality in 2025
Jurassic Pharaohs: Unlocking the Magick of Ancient Egypt and Dino Wicca
The Happiness Equation: Small Changes for Big Joy
The Confidence Compass: Finding Your Inner Strength
Whispers in the Hollow: Tales of the Forgotten Beasts
Echoes from the Hollow: The Return of Forgotten Beasts
The Hollow Ascendant: The Rise of the Forgotten Beasts
The Relationship Reset: Building Better Connections
Mastering the Morning: How to Win the Day Before 8 AM
The Shadow's Dance: Groundhog Day Symbolism
Cupid's Kitchen: Quick Valentine's Day Recipes
Valentine's Day on a Budget: Love Without Breaking the Bank
Astrocraft: Aligning the Stars in the World of Minecraft
Forecasting Life: Groundhog Day Reflections

Bleeding Hearts: Twisted Tales of Valentine's Terror

Herbal Smoke Revolution: The Ultimate Guide to Nature's Cigarette Alternative

Winter's Wrath: The Complete Survival Blueprint for Extreme Freezes.

The Groundhog's Shadow: A Tale of Seasons
Burrowed Insights: Wisdom from the Groundhog

Sensual Strings: The Art of Erotic Bondage
Whispered Flames: Unlocking the Power of Fire Play
Forgotten Shadows: A Guide to Cryptids Lost to Time
Six Weeks of Secrets: Groundhog Day's Hidden Messages
Shadows and Cycles: Groundhog Day Reflections
The Art of Love Letters: Crafting the Perfect Message
Romantic Getaways at Home: Turning Your Space into Paradise
Purrfect Brews: A Cat Lover's Guide to Coffee and Companionship
The Groundhog's Wisdom: Timeless Lessons for Modern Life
The Shadow Oracle: Groundhog Day as a Predictor
Emerging from the Burrow: A Journey of Renewal
The Language of Love: Learning Your Partner's Love Style
Authorpreneur: The Ultimate Blueprint for Writing, Publishing, and Thriving as an Author
Weathering the Seasons: Groundhog Day Perspectives
Valentine's Day Magic: A Guide to Romantic Rituals
The Shadow Chronicles: Stories of Groundhog Day
Love and Laughter: Fun Games for Valentine's Day
AstroRealty: Unlocking the Stars for Property Success
The Groundhog's Path: A Guide to Seasonal Balance
Groundhog Day Diaries: Reflections in the Shadow
The Groundhog's Light: Illuminating the Path Ahead
Valentine's Traditions from Around the World
AI Wealth Revolution: Unlocking the Trillionaire Mindset
Love Rekindled: Reigniting Passion in Relationships
Single and Thriving: Self-Love on Valentine's Day
Emerald Legends: Mystical Tales of Ireland
Green Alchemy: Harnessing Nature's Magic
The Hearts of Horror: A Valentine's Day Nightmare
The Leprechaun's Guide to Wealth and Wisdom
Dancing with the Sidhe: Celebrating the Otherworld

Shamrocks and Shadows: Mysteries of the Green Isle

Emerald Energy: Harnessing Luck and Growth

The Gingerbread Golem's Valentine: A Sweetheart's Guide to Love and Enchantment

The Celtic Knot: Weaving Life and Destiny

Green Fire: Elemental Magic for St. Patrick's Day

Clover Chronicles: Finding Your Inner Luck

Ireland's Mystical Creatures: A Field Guide

Gingerbread Golem's Love Almanac

Prowl and Thrive: The Lion's Guide to Success

Love Alchemy: Transforming Your Life Through Heart Energy

WORLD DOMINATION: Woman's Rule 3:The New Life

The Midnight Rose: A Guide to Lunar Love Spells

The Forbidden Letters: Writing Your Own Love Prophecy

Luck and Lore: St. Patrick's Day for Modern Mystics

The Green Path: A Pagan Celebration of Renewal

The Dark Architect's Guide to Reprogramming Reality

Prankster's Paradise: A Guide to Harmless Hijinks

Manifest Your Reality: The Law of Attraction Simplified

The TARDIS Owner's Manual: Understanding the Doctor's Ship: *A complete guide to the TARDIS, its technology, secrets, and mysteries*

Starlit Romance: Astrology Secrets for Finding True Love

The Time Lord's Atlas: A Complete Guide to the Whoniverse: ***A breakdown of the locations, planets, and dimensions explored in Doctor Who***

Sweetheart Shadows: The Dark Side of Love and Attraction

February Fire: Reigniting Passion in Every Area of Life

The Self-Love Toolkit: 5 Ways to Embrace Who You Are

February Sparks: Ignite Your Dreams in 28 Days

March to Success: A 31-Day Action Blueprint

Ancient Paths: The 13 Sacred Principles of Dino Wicca

Echoes of Tomorrow: Navigating the AI Revolution
The Wellness Blueprint: Balancing Mind, Body, and Soul
Green Horizons: Sustainable Living for a Better Tomorrow
The AI Wealth Code: How to Make Millions with Automation
AI-Powered Creativity: Writing, Art, and Music for Profit
Extinction Rites: Rebirthing Your Soul Through Prehistoric Magick
Sacred Serpents tarot
Celestial Enchantment blank journal
Star Strains
Culinary Journeys: Exploring Global Flavors at Home
The Hollowvale Curse
The Hollowvale Harvest
The Egg of Transformation: Awakening Your Inner Power
Blooming Into Power: A Wiccan Guide to Spring Awakening
The Nightmare Nexus: The Third Doctor's Perilous Haunting
Digital Detox: Reclaiming Your Life in a Connected World
Ostara's Path: Walking the Spiral of Renewal
The Sacred Hare
Financial Freedom: Building Wealth in the Modern Age
Spring's Cauldron: Stirring the Waters of Change
The Hollowvale Pact
Quantum Consciousness: The Science of Reality Shifting
The Hollowvale Hunger
The Sacred Waters Within: A Witch's Guide to Hydrocephalus Magick
The Raven's Nest: Building a Life of Unshakable Stability
AI and the Human Mind: The Future of Intelligence
The Hollowvale Reckoning
Timeless Love: Building and Maintaining Lasting Relationships
The Raven's Roar: Unlocking Unstoppable Confidence
Raven Sight: Awakening Intuition and Inner Wisdom

The Butterfly Effect: Small Changes, Big Transformations

Taming the Boogeyman: How to Conquer Your Inner Fears

The Magick of Green: Awakening Earth's Energy in You

The Entrepreneurial Mindset: Secrets to Business Success

The Hollowvale End

The Shadow Luck Ritual: Reclaiming Power from Your Dark Side

Spring Magick for Beginners: A Simple Guide to Seasonal Energy Work

Doctor Who: The Hollowvale Conundrum

The March of Miracles: Unlocking Synchronicities in Spring

Unveiling the Cosmos: A Guide to Stargazing and Space Exploration

The Ultimate Guide to Surviving an Economic Collapse

The AI Gold Rush: How to Profit from the AI Revolution

Bastet's Shadow: The Hidden Power of Feline Magick

The Bastet Codex: Unlocking the Goddess's Magickal Secrets

Purring Spells: Harnessing Bastet's Healing Frequencies

Bastet's Nine Lives: Rebirth, Transformation, and Immortality Spells

Primal Currents: Hydrocephalus Magick in the Path of Dino Wicca

The Digital Gold Rush: Mastering E-Commerce and Online Sales

Future Shock: Adapting to the Next Decade of Change

The Quantum Mindset: Think Like a Billionaire

Sacred Motherhood: Awakening the Divine Feminine Within

The Mother's Spellbook: Enchantments for Love, Protection, and Prosperity

The Witch's Guide to Parenting: Raising Empowered and Intuitive Children

The Magick of Motherhood: Reclaiming Your Power Through Rituals

The Pagan Path to Self-Love: A Goddess's Guide to Worth and Confidence
Wild Woman Magick: Unleashing Your Primal Power
The Money Magnet Blueprint: Unlocking Unlimited Wealth
Biohacking 101: Unlock Your Body's Full Potential
The Wild Father: A Pagan Guide to Strength and Wisdom
The Sacred Masculine: Unlocking Your Inner Power
The Druid's Compass
The Warrior's Mindset
The Father's Fire
Odin's Path
Ancestral Bonds
The House That Whispers
The Magician's Code
The Wild Hunt
The Green Man's Path
The Altar of Success
The Shadow and the Sword
The High Priestess's Guide to Energy Healing
The Lunar Mother
The Sacred Self-Care Grimoire
The Womb Wisdom Codex
The Wheel of the Mother
The Witch's Guide to Manifestation
The Q2 Reset
The Ultimate Guide to AI-Powered Passive Income
Escape the 9-5
AI Feline Fortunes
The Tear-Stained Grimoire
Razorblade Runes
Cemetery Sirens
The Midnight Wristwatch
The Town That Forgets

AI Horror & Creepypasta
The Hollow Frequency
The Breach Echo
The Quiet Between Worlds
The Sigil of Tharan-Khul
Summon the Vault of Y'ha'ten
The Becoming Codex
The Profit of Az'ra-nar
The Drowned Logos
Echoes of the Eldritch Will
The Deep Ledger
Necronomicon of Networth
Covenant of the Wealthwyrm
The Whisperer's Manifesto
The Rites of Azh-K'luth
The Ark of the Crawling Coin
The Tithe of Shadows
Inkheart Abyss
The Timewinds of Y'ha-nthlei
The Spiral Labyrinth of Azag-Nirrh
The Gallifreyan Heresy of the Black Pharaoh
The Psalms of Nyog-Sotha
Black Rain Alchemy
The Infinite Maw
The Entropic Blueprint
The Oracle of Sh'guul
The Book of Breach
The Drowned Saint's Testament
Dreamcraft of the Sleeper God
The Silence Market
Cthonomics: The Dark Wealth Algorithm
Invocation of the Ten-Eyed King
Wealthbound to the Wyrm Below

Become the Unnameable
Codex of the Sovereign Flame
Rituals of Relentless Becoming
The Shadow Ascends
The Eyes Beneath You
The Will That Wakes Worlds
Silence Is a Weapon
The Mirror That Screams
The Whisper Between Moments
The Mind That Devours Fear
The Myth of the Finished Self
The Architect of Your Madness
The Voice You've Buried
The Discipline of Madness
Stormborn: Awakening Your Inner Tempest
The Mind That Ate Time
Unbind Your Becoming
The Pact You Owe Yourself
The Devourer's Diet
The Acid That Carves the Path
The Tower You Must Burn
The Breath Between Worlds
Speak Like the Deep
The Labyrinth Within
The Spine of the Sea God
Rejection Is a Portal
The Crown You Refused
The Scar Is the Spell
The Lightless Flame
The Habit of Becoming Horrific
ChickenJockey Chaos
The Gatekeeper Within
You Are Not Your Name

The Compass of the Mad
The Archive of Unsent Letters
What the Mirror Can't Show You
The Knife You Needed
Worship Nothing, Become Everything
The Other Voice
The Body the World Forgot
The Vein of the Void
The Black Bone Codex
The Puzzle of the Hidden Self (Millennium Puzzle)
The Eye That Sees the Lie *(Millennium Eye)*
The Ring of Return (Millennium Ring)
The Rod of Relentless Will *(Millennium Rod)*
The Tally of the Soul (Millennium Tauk/Necklace)
The Key to the Locked Timeline (Millennium Key)
The Scale of Sacred Decisions (Millennium Scales)
Inferno Bites: The UnOfficial Minecraft Lava Cookbook
Rot in the Attic
Prana: The Hidden Force of Your Infinite Self
The Shadow Realm Within: Transforming Darkness Into Destiny
The Borderland Collapse
Claws of Protection: Bastet's Defensive Magick
Mr. Ring-a-Ding's Madness
Yugioh Astrology: Celestial Deckcraft and Duel Destiny (2026–2027 Edition)
The Seal You Signed: Unlocking the Power You Once Feared
The Puzzle of Infinite Minds: Unlocking the Mentalism Hidden Within
The Eye That Mirrors the All: Secrets of Inner Reflection
Doctor Who: The Toymaker's Broadcast
The Rod of Eternal Flow: Commanding the Currents of Vibration

Golden Eyes of Bastet: Enhancing Psychic Vision
The Key of Dual Forces: Balance Within the Polarity
The Scales of Living Rhythm: Timing the Dance of Life
The Necklace of Hidden Cause: Weaving the Webs of Fate
The Ring of Secret Masters: Rising Through the All Within All
Daggers of the Dying Deep
Bastet's Wealth and Fortune Magick: Prosperity Rituals of the Goddess
The Tide that Speaks
The Scrolls of Petosiris: 13 Rituals from the Feathered Eye
Petosiris and the Living Plague of Osirion
Feline Fire: Bastet's Passion and Love Magick
The Star Altar of Petosiris
Bastet's Whiskers: Supernatural Sensory Magick
The Bastet Grimoire
Feeding the Shadows
The Mouthless Prayer
The Spiral Wound
Becoming the Ibis: Lessons from Petosiris's Mind
The Crimson Coven: Cola Magick for Sweet Dominion
Sacred Cat's Paw
The Soda Zodiac: A Flavor for Every Sign
Covenant of the Crawling Flame
The Ink of Ish'Zur
Frothroot: The Thirst That Ate the World
The Golden Glyphs of Prosperity
The Etherbind Codex
Echoes of the Resistance: Reclaiming the You That Survived
Harnessed Minds: Breaking Free from Mental Control
The Eyes in the Smoke
Rootwake: The Carbon Covenant
Skitter Logic: Unlearning the Fear That Built You

Doctor Who: The World That Froths
Rootwake: The Fizz That Rewrites Flesh
Rootwake: Frothfather of the World
The Holly Pact: Blood Beneath the Mistletoe
The 2nd Mass Principle: Building Unbreakable Tribes
Web of Wits: A Survival Guide to Encounters with Anasi the Spider (Aunt Nancy)
The Hexbreaking Handbook: Effective Spells to Remove Curses
Pop Alchemy: Transform Your Life One Sip at a Time
The Mason Code: Leading in Unleadable Times
Petosiris and the Fifth Chamber of Thoth
The Ether Seed Within
The Parent of Tomorrow
Petosiris's Pyramid of Perpetual Wealth
Unlearn the World
Grimoire of the Hollow Tongue
Zodiac Weeds: Finding Your Strain Through the Stars
Aquarius Rises in the Bank
The Sugar God's Smile
The Skinclock Reversal: Biohacking the Face of Time
Debtburn: How to Obliterate What You Owe Forever
The Ice Cream Oracle: What Your Cone Says About Your Future
Silence Is Sovereignty: The Power of Being Unreadable
The Wind That Whispers Through Stone
Path of the Four Directions
Doctor Who: The Maestro's Symphony of Endings
Oxygen Grail: Breathing to Undo the Clock
Zodiacal Collapse: When Stars Devour Time
Teachings from the Red Sand Silence
Doctor Who: Omega – The Broken Equation
Memory Wipe Your Past: Start Over Like a MiB

Mitochondria Prime: Ignite the Core of Youth

A Nest of Roaches

Grub from the Galaxy: MiB Recipes You'll Never Forget

Whiskers of Power: Bastet's Guide to Inner Sovereignty

The Gift Must Cost Them: Negotiation Through Unequal Exchange

The Worm Guys' Wealth Code: Hustle Like an Alien

Bug Out: The Edgar Method for Ruthless Goal Setting

Weaving Life with Spiderwoman's Pattern

Doctor Who: The Rani's Renaissance

How to Get a Job (If You're a Puppygirl)

Speak Through Others: The Art of Proxy Power

T-Rex Your Trauma: Reclaim the Power of Your Primal Self

The Black Briefcase: How MiB Stay Wealthy in Silence

The Thirst Beyond Reason: Understanding Diabetes Insipidus From the Inside Out

Backwoods Witchcraft for Billionaires: The Pagan Path from Dirt Roads to Gold Roads

The Moonshine Grimoire: Fermented Spells for Abundance

The Nameless Geometry

The Wraith's Mixtape: Spellcasting with Songs of Sorrow

The Gallifreyan Gentleman: Silent Wealth, Sonic Confidence, and the Doctor's Code of Living

Sugar Water Confidence

Dino Totems: Spirit Guides from Earth's First Gods

Pumpkin Sigils & Ritual Smoke

The Hózhó Compass

The Distortus Discipline – Order from Inner Mutation

Witchcraft for the Cold-Blooded Soul

Moonlight Over the Blessingway

Water, Interrupted: When the Body Forgets How to Hold On

Deformed but Divine: Embracing Your Asymmetry

Hexes in the Henhouse: The Farm Witch's Guide to Power

The Reversed Flame: A Grimoire of Inverted Power

Salt, Cells, and Sanity: Reclaiming Balance with Diabetes Insipidus

King of the Broken: Crowning the Flawed Self

Moonlight Scars: Emo Moon Magick and the Art of Lunar Sorrow

Noose Spells: Magick of the Hanging Rope

The Goth Cathedral: Rituals of the Broken and Beautiful

The Cretaceous Codex: Dino Spirits and Fossil Magick

The Turkey Bones Ritual

Nine Lives of Manifestation: Unlocking Bastet's Reality Codes

Chaos Muscles: Building Strength from Twisted Pain

Emo Blood Magick: The Veins of Power

The 3AM Flood: Nighttime Urination, Sleep Loss, and the DI Spiral

The Silence Between the Stars

The Lemon Method: Sour Your Way to Success

Starlit Sovereign

The Rite of Twelve Gates: Walking the Gates of the Duat.

Cornbread and Conjure: Recipes for Riches and Rootwork

The Black Rose Rituals: Emo Love Spells and Obsession Magick

The Eternal Goodbye: Death Magick and Rebirth Rituals

Sinkrot: The Drain That Remembers

The Hybrid Mindset: Thinking Beyond Evolution

Bone Dry: Navigating Dehydration Before It Breaks You

Wreathcraft: Winter Sigils and Yuletide Spells

The Rite of Twelve Mouths

S'mores of the Damned: Haunted Recipes for Halloween Night

Rethink the Drink: A Beverage Survival Guide for DI Warriors

The Shadow Chord: Guitar Magick and Sonic

Malformed Yet Majestic: Leading When You Feel Wrong Inside

The Cursed Diary: Ink-Stained Spells of the Emo Soul

Anxiety Off Switch: Emergency Reset for a Fried Nervous System

The Energy Heist: How to Take Back Your Life from Drainers

Beyond the Bathroom: Rebuilding Your Social Life With DI

Coyote's Gift for Decision Makers

Ghoul-Goo: Spooky S'mores You'll Die For

Echoes in the Mirror: Scrying and Self-Destruction Magick

Thread and Thorn: Stitching Spells from Rural Cloth

The Mogwai Mind: Building Untouchable Wealth from Small Ideas

Be Your Own Guide: Trust Your Inner Compass

Hormones in Chaos: The Endocrine Puzzle of Diabetes Insipidus

ChronoCleanse: Detox Your Biological Timeline

The Limb You Hide Is the One That Saves You

Leaves, Bones, and Whisper Spells

The Dinosaur Mindset: Prehistoric Tactics for Modern Wealth

Clawing Back Control: A Bastet Method for Boundaries and Empowerment

Samhain Codes of the Forgotten

Orange Alchemy: The Autumnal Spellbook

Monster Within, Master Without

The Sigil That Sleeps

Hearthcraft: Yule Hearth Sigils and Winter Warmth Spells

Temple of the Purring Moon: Rituals from Bastet's Lineage

When the Earth Remembers Your Footsteps

Food for Mood: Eat to Heal Depression, Not Just Survive It

Witch of the Kudzu Vine: Southern Pagan Wealth Secrets

The Invisible Diagnosis: Advocating for Yourself With DI

The Coffin's Lullaby: Sleep Magick and Nightmares as Portals
Ashes of the Will: Rituals for Erasing the Self
The Fracture Rite: Shattering the Magickal Core
Funeral Candles: The Art of Emo Flame Magick
The Black Grimoire: A Blank Ritual for Writing in Absence
Phantom Thirst: A Halloween Survival Guide for Diabetes Insipidus
The Hollow Crown: Emo Royalty and Magick of the Outcast King
Sandpainting for the Soul
Falling Into Balance: Using the Extra Hour to Recalibrate Life
100 Southern Superstitions That Still Work
The DI Child: A Parent's Guide to Raising Hydrated, Happy Kids
The Jungle of Shame: Escaping the Hidden Lab of Doubt
The Witch's Toast: S'mores Spells and Creepy Confections
The Hoodoo Pantry: Spells from the Mason Jar
The Immortal Fortune: Secret Wealth Lessons from Captain Jack Harkness
The Specter's Embrace: Magick for Channeling Ghostly Lovers
Grateful Waters: A Thanksgiving Survival Guide for Diabetes Insipidus
The Seizure Gospel
Harvestbind: Autumn Sigils and Samhain Spells
Doctor Who: The Algorithmic Awakening
Silent Nights, Steady Waters: A Christmas Survival Guide for Diabetes Insipidus
The Extra Hour Effect: How One Hour Can Transform Everything
Blade Between the Breaths
Running with the Mountain Shadows
Echoes of the Failed Experiment – Becoming a Living Legacy

Swamp Witches & River Ghosts: Real Southern Hauntings

Cornbread Prophecies: Magical Recipes from a Southern Table

Doctor Who: The Signal in the Star

Bloomcraft: Spring Sigils and Equinox Enchantments

Vanisher: How to Disappear from the Internet Without Losing Your Life

The Ultimate Christmas Cookie Cookbook

The Unbreakable Parent: How to Mentally Survive Raising Kids in a Broken World

Time Debt: How to Reclaim the Hours You Didn't Know You Lost

One Month, One Million: Unconventional Cash Creation Tactics

Doctor Who: The Cyber Conversion Protocol

Black Friday Frenzy: The Art of Finding Hidden Online Deals

The Grimoire Buried Under the Apple Tree

Digital Couponing Masterclass: Your Step-by-Step Guide to Black Friday Savings

The Fire Inside the Flint

Shadows on the Ceiling: The Emo Guide to Astral Magick

The Bone-Eaters Beneath Us

Black Friday Bundle Blueprint: Creating Irresistible Product Packages for Maximum Sales

Thirteen Nights of Unbinding

Doctor Who: Engines of Influence

Pumpkin Spice Alchemy: Recipes of Fire and Frost

When Raptor Met Rexy: Prehistoric Lessons in Wild Romance

Oblivion's Candle: Burn the Path Behind You

Campfire Curses and Chocolate: A Halloween S'mores Grimoire

The Wallet That Wasn't Mine: Breaking Free from Inherited Scarcity

The Cola Zodiac: What Your Fizz Says About Your Fate

Frostfire Fortune: Unlocking Winter's Hidden Prosperity

Signal Jamming: Detox Your Brain from Info Overload

The Dust of the Forgotten Rite

The Golden Cat Sigils: Drawing Power in Bastet's Name

Mud Magick: The Prosperity of Getting Dirty

Savory Spicefall: Beyond the Pumpkin Pie

Pumpkin Spice Apothecary Kitchen

The Pumpkin Spice Economy: Turning Trends into Billions

The Ember Veil: 13 Nights of Fire Magick

Financial Freeze: When Earning Triggers Panic

The Gingerbread Alchemist: Sweet Recipes with a Twist

Biosynth Power: Programming Yourself from Scratch

Echoes from the Talking Circle

Truffle Alchemy: Fungus of Fortune

Spores of Power: The Truffle Witch's Handbook

Doctor Who: The Tower That Speaks

The Mycelium Veil: Truffle Magick Unbound

Broke But Ashamed: Healing the Shame Wound of Debt

The Evergreen Mind: Growth Through Winter Stillness

The Black Veil Truffle Rite

The Voice Beneath Symbols

Witchlight on the Bayou: Swamp Spells for Sovereignty

I Grew Up Poor and Now I Sabotage My Success

The Lantern of Hollow Souls

Shutdown Survival: A Citizen's Guide to Thriving When Government Stops

When Abundance Feels Like a Threat: Healing the Hidden Fears of Enough

The Scarecrow Grimoire

Owls of the October Veil

Candlewax and Curses: A Halloween Spellbook

Excavating the Inner Fossil – Transforming Fossilized Thoughtforms into Tools of Power

The Yule Witch's Spellbook: Magick for the Holiday Season

Haunted Christmas: Ghost Stories for Winter Nights

The Christmas Survival Guide: Thriving Through the Chaos

The Bone Orchard Rites

Haunted Commerce: The Ghost in the Marketplace

When Money Triggers the Inner Child

Silent Night with the Silence: A Christmas Thriller

The Lightning Crown: Living and Leading Through Seizures

TARDIS Tidings: Festive Stories from the Whoniverse

Autumn Reset: Slowing Down Without Falling Behind

The Trillion Dollar Soul: Rewriting the Currency of Reality

Truffle Eclipse Magick

Micro-Manifestations: Quick Magick That Works

5-Minute Rituals for Busy Witches

The Marshmallow Massacre: Halloween Treats with a Sinister Twist

Blood and Blackberry Thorns

Magickal Mornings: Rituals for a Blessed Christmas Day

Embers of the All-Hallows Fire

The Pumpkin Market Collapse

The Hour You Gained: Transforming Time Into Power

The Chamber Must Be Sealed: Mastering the Power of Controlled Access

The Cursed Manuscript of Petosiris

The Festive Hearth: Creating Holiday Traditions

Darkness Rising: Thriving as Nights Grow Longer

Harvesting Time: Turning the Year's End Into Your New Beginning

Petosiris and the 13th Zodiac Key

Wagewound: When Paychecks Become Identity Prisons

Walls That Watch

The Silent Feast: Rituals of Power in the Longest Night

The Distortus Legacy : Becoming a Deformed King in a Perfect World

The Hollow Masks

The Gratitude Furnace: Forging Gold from Thanks

Feast of Inner Gold: Eating for Energy and Enlightenment

Haunted Commerce: The Season of Spending Spirits

Fear Bonds: How Panic Creates Profit

Black Friday E-Commerce Playbook: Sales Tactics to Skyrocket Your Holiday Revenue

Budgeting for Black Friday: A Holiday Savings Planner

Haunting the Harvest Moon

The Warrior's Water: Emergency Preparedness for People With DI

The First Sip of the Year: A New Year's Survival Guide for Diabetes Insipidus

Doctor Who: The Thirteenth Node

The Unseen Struggle: Mental Health, Anxiety, and Chronic Thirst

The Hearth's Hidden Ledger: Counting Energies as Currency

The Gift Alchemist: Turning Any Offering Into Gold

The Papyrus of the Bound Spirit

The Magick of Leftovers: Transmutation in the Fridge

Frost and Fortune: Christmas Wealthcraft for the Modern Magus

Last-Minute Gifts: Creative Ideas on a Budget

10 Secrets to Surviving Holiday Crowds

The Witch's Dow Jones

The Witches' Graveyard Shift

Pumpkin Sigils: Carving Rites for Midnight Power

The Secret Shopper's Black Friday Guide: How to Get Early Access and VIP Deals

Fever in the Foundation

The Neuralyzer Reset: Reprogram Your Morning Routine

Lightning Lessons of the White Painted Woman

The Enchanted Snowflake

The Magic Sip: Surviving Disney Parks with Diabetes Insipidus

The One Who Draws Through You

Santa's Secrets: A Magical Holiday Planner

Silent Bells, Loud Miracles: Self-Help for the Season of Stillness

The Sugar Spell Codex: Confectionary Magick of Christmas

Autumn Hexcraft: Fallen Leaves, Fallen Barriers

Sleep Like a Fortress: Build a Life Where Insomnia Can't Survive

Nowhere Was Ever Home

Christmas Under the Stars: A Celestial Holiday Guide

Rentproof: How to Never Be Evicted Again

Workless: Escape the 9-5 Without Being Broke

The Gilded Gift: A Wealth Altar for Christmas Morning

The Black Friday Grimoire

The Hollowing: Ceremonies of Spiritual Collapse

Doctor Who: The Nameless Signal

Where the Eagle Hides His Courage

The Dwarf Tyrant's Ascent: Claiming Power in a World of Giants

The Currency of the Dead: Trading with Spectral Bankers

The Icebound Witch: Survival and Magick in the Cold

The Emergency Money Mind: Constant Crisis, Zero Calm

Thirst & Roses: A Valentine's Survival Guide for Diabetes Insipidus

Springing Into Clarity: Mastering the Energy Shift of Daylight Saving

Speed of the Nanotyrant: Agile Strategies for Life's Hunt

The 90-Day Reset: A Science-Backed Guide to Reinvent Yourself Before the New Year

The Coil of Thorns

Timegates Unleashed

Dopamine Fasting 2.0: Rewiring Your Brain in a World of Overstimulation

The Nanotyrannus Mutation: Embracing Your Differentiated Form

Unwritten January: How to Use the Blank Page of the Year to Re-Author Your Life

Feast of the Forgotten Spirits: Ancestor Magick for the Holidays

The Burnout Codex: A System for Thriving Beyond Stress

I Don't Deserve to Have Money

When the King Doesn't See You: The Shadow Predator's Guide

The Reset Ritual :A Guide to Shedding Last Year's Weight—Emotional and Physical—by Spring Cleaning Your Soul

Calendar Alchemy: Learn to Bend Time and Productivity around Your Natural Rhythms

The Mirror Contract: A One-Sentence Agreement with Yourself that Unlocks Real Change

The Nile Formula: Sacred Flow for Millionaire Minds

Forward Momentum: Productivity Rituals for the Lost Hour

Harvest Gold: Wealth Magick of Pumpkin Spice Commerce

The Magick of Christmas Lights: Illuminating Holiday Rituals

Cranberry Crown: Royal Self-Worth through Ritual Meals

Petosiris and the Worms of the Feathered Throne

The Evergreen Equation: Self-Help for Sustained Growth

The Rain Will Wash Us Away: Emo Weather Magick

Snowlight Shadows: Magick Under Frozen Stars

Doctor Who: Merger of Empires

The Light Within the Feast: Magickal Wealth of Yuletide Flame

Momentum Machines: Small Habits Designed to Snowball into Unstoppable Forward Motion

Calm Spells: Magickal Solutions for Anxiety Relief

Santa's Final List: The Naughty Never Leave

The Mystic's Guide to Banishing Worry

The Silence Dividend: Turning Quiet Mornings into Compounding Growth All Year

Charmed Stillness: Rituals to Ease the Mind

Blood Spiral Ascension

The Vanishing Heart Invocation

Crystal Calm: Harnessing Stones for Anxiety

The Nano Tyrant Code: Strength in the Small Predator

The Energy Ledger: Accounting Methods for Vitality, Not Just Money

Snowglobe Mindset: Shake Up Your Thoughts, Settle Into Peace

The Weight of the Feather: Anubis's Codes for Soul Balance

Pocket Peppermint Power: Tiny Rituals for Big Holiday Energy

Shadowkeeper of the Golden Jackal: Anubis's Path to Energetic Protection

The Witch's Breath: Anxiety Relief Through Magickal Breathing

The Tiny Ember: Pocket Motivation for Cold Days

Stocking Sorcery: Mini Spells for Holiday Luck and Prosperity

Warm Hands, Steady Heart: Micro Grounding for Winter Anxiety

The Jackal's Lantern: Guide-Lights for Walking the Dark Path

Anubis's Silent Steps: Rituals for Stealth, Peace & Emotional Quiet

The Bonewake Protocol

Extinction-Proof: How to Outlive Trends, Trauma, and Time

The Fourth Doctor: The Eccentric Wanderer

The Second Doctor: Chaos and Charm in the TARDIS (Patrick Troughton, 1966–1969)

The Third Doctor: Earthbound Defender of Time (Jon Pertwee, 1970–1974)

The First Doctor: Genesis of the Time Lord (William Hartnell, 1963–1966)

The Fourth Doctor: The Eccentric Wanderer ***(Tom Baker, 1974–1981)***

The Fifth Doctor: Elegance and Empathy (Peter Davison, 1982–1984)

The Sixth Doctor: A Kaleidoscope of Conflict (Colin Baker, 1984–1986)

The Seventh Doctor: The Strategist of Shadows (Sylvester McCoy, 1987–1989)

The Eighth Doctor: A Time Lord's Renaissance (Paul McGann, 1996)

The War Doctor: A Time Lord's Burden (John Hurt, 2013)

The Ninth Doctor: The Healer of Worlds ***(Christopher Eccleston, 2005)***

The Tenth Doctor: The Lonely Hero (David Tennant, 2005–2010)

The Eleventh Doctor: The Madman in a Box (Matt Smith, 2010–2013)

The Twelfth Doctor: The Rebel with a Cause (Peter Capaldi, 2013–2017)

The Thirteenth Doctor: Breaking the Mold **(Jodie Whittaker, 2017–2022)**

The Fourteenth Doctor: A New Beginning (David Tennant, 2022–2023)

The Fifteenth Doctor: Rewriting the Stars
(Ncuti Gatwa, 2023–2025)

Santa's Shortcut to Success: Micro Habits for a Better New Year

The Midnight Cocoa Manifesto: Comfort Rituals for Hard Nights

Get Some Tarot cards: https://www.makeplayingcards.com/sell/apophis-occult-shop

Get some shirts: https://www.bonfire.com/store/apophis-shirt-emporium/

<u>Instagrams:</u>
@apophis_enterprises,
@apophisbookemporium,
@apophisscardshop
Twitter: @apophisenterpr1
Tiktok:@apophisenterprise
Youtube: @sg1fan23477
Hive: @sg1fan23477
CheeLee: @SG1fan23477

Podcast: Apophis Chat Zone: https://open.spotify.com/show/5zXbrCLEV2xzCp8ybrfHsk?si=fb4d4fdbdce44dec

Newsletter: https://apophiss-newsletter-27c897.beehiiv.com/

If you want to support me or see posts of other projects that I have come over to: **buymeacoffee.com/mpetchinskg**

I post there daily several times a day

Get your Dinowicca or Christmas themed digital products, especially Santa Raptor songs and other musics. Here: **https://sg1fan23477.gumroad.com**

Apophis Yuletide Digital has not only digital Christmas items, but it will have all things with Dinowicca as well as other Digital products.

www.ingramcontent.com/pod-product-compliance
Lightning Source LLC
LaVergne TN
LVHW022226200926
848481LV00006B/2142
9798330611829